CRYPTO SIMPLIFIED

CRYPTO SIMPLIFIED

THE ULTIMATE BEGINNERS GUIDE TO UNDERSTANDING CRYPTOCURRENCY

NADAV SANANES

Nadav Sananes

Crypto Simplified

The Ultimate Beginners Guide To Understanding Cryptocurrency

Published by Spines
ISBN: 979-8-90222-279-8

DEDICATION

To the Creator — thank You for the blessings, guidance, and strength that made this journey possible.

Dedicated to everyone taking their first step into the world of crypto —

May this book guide you with clarity, confidence, and curiosity.

To my family — thank you for your endless support, love, and belief in me throughout this journey.

To Netanel, — thank you for helping shape the process, building and managing the site, and supporting the vision every step of the way.

To the incredible team at Spines — thank you for helping bring this project together so beautifully, and for your continuous support, guidance, and dedication throughout the entire process.

DISCLAIMER

This book is **not financial advice**. It's here to **educate and inform**, not to tell you what to buy or sell. Crypto can be exciting, but it's also risky—prices can swing wildly, and you could lose all your money. **Do your own research**, make your own choices, and enter the crypto world **at your own risk**. We are not paid to promote or shill any token or project.

CONTENTS

About CryptoCube xiii
Message from the author xv

CHAPTER 1: INTRODUCTION TO CRYPTO 1
Welcome to the World of Cryptocurrency 1
The Evolution of Money: From Shells to Satoshi 2
The Birth of Bitcoin 3
What Is Cryptocurrency, Really? 4
How a Blockchain Works—Plainly 5
Why Crypto Matters Now 6
First Steps, First Safeguards 7
The Design Choices: Energy, Speed, and Trade-Offs 7
What the Ecosystem Looks Like 8
The Culture: Open-Source, Open Discussion 9
Common Misconceptions 9
A Realistic View of Risk 10
The Broader Vision 10
Where We Go Next 11

CHAPTER 2: CRYPTO BASICS 12
What Exactly Is Crypto? 12
Understanding Crypto Wallets 13
How Transactions Work 15
Mining and Validation 16
Public vs. Private Blockchains 16
A Deeper Look at Ethereum 17
Everyday Uses of Crypto 18
The Rise of Altcoins 18
Building Toward the Next Step 19

CHAPTER 3: FUNDAMENTALS 20
Decentralization: Power Spread Out 21
Cryptography: The Science of Security 22
Supply, Demand, and Scarcity 24

Consensus Mechanisms: Reaching Agreement Without Trust 25
Ethereum's Merge: A Case Study 26
Tokenomics: The Economics of Tokens 27
Risks and Challenges 28
Building Up to the Next Chapter 29

CHAPTER 4: WHY BLOCKCHAIN IS SO AWESOME 30
The Hidden Engine Behind Cryptocurrency 30
A Story of Shared Truth 31
How a Blockchain Actually Works 31
Why Blockchain Is a Big Deal 32
Beyond Money: Real-World Use Cases 34
Success Stories and Experiments 35
Challenges and Criticisms 36
The Big Picture: The Internet of Value 37
Closing Thoughts 37

CHAPTER 5: THE MAIN CRYPTOCURRENCIES 39
Meeting the Giants of the Crypto World 39
Bitcoin (BTC): Scarcity with a Spine 40
Litecoin (LTC): The Silver to Bitcoin's Gold 41
Namecoin (NMC): The First Experiment Beyond Money 42
Peercoin (PPC): Early Steps Toward Sustainability 42
XRP Ledger (XRP): Speeding Up the Plumbing of Finance 43
Ethereum (ETH): The World Computer 44
BNB Chain (BNB): From Exchange Token to Ecosystem Powerhouse 45
Cardano (ADA): Science Meets Blockchain 46
Solana (SOL): The Speed Demon 46
Polkadot (DOT): The Multichain Vision 47
Choosing Tools, Not Sides 48
Closing Thoughts 49

CHAPTER 6: THE BEST CRYPTO APPS AND EXCHANGES 50
Entering the World of Crypto Tools 50
Why Apps and Exchanges Matter 51
The Role of Cryptocurrency Exchanges 51
Building Your Crypto Toolkit 53
Case Studies: The Apps That Shaped Adoption 54
Security and Best Practices 56
How Beginners Can Build Confidence 56
Closing Thoughts 57

CHAPTER 7: HOW TO BUY AND SELL CRYPTO 58
Taking the Leap 58
Before You Buy: Preparing the Ground 59
Method 1: Buying Through a Centralized Exchange 60
Method 2: Buying Peer-to-Peer (P2P) 61
Method 3: Buying via Wallet Apps 61
Selling Cryptocurrency: Exiting the Market 62
Common Pitfalls to Avoid 62
A Practical Walkthrough: Your First Purchase 63
Selling Scenario 64
The Bigger Picture 64
Key Takeaways 65
Preparing for What's Next 65

CHAPTER 8: TRADING AND HOLDING 66
Two Paths, One Goal 66
The Nature of the Crypto Market 67
Trading: The Active Path 67
Holding (HODLing): The Passive Path 70
Trading vs. Holding: A Comparison 72
A Hybrid Approach 73
Lessons from History 73
Key Takeaways 74
Building Toward the Next Chapter 74

CHAPTER 9: CRYPTO SECURITY 75
Why Security is the Cornerstone of Crypto 75
The Landscape of Crypto Threats 76

Common Scams and Hacks in Crypto 76
Best Practices for Crypto Security 80
The Human Factor 82
Lessons from History 82
Building Toward the Final Chapter 83

CHAPTER 10: YOUR CRYPTO JOURNEY BEGINS 84
The Road So Far 84
Crypto as a Journey, Not a Destination 85
Building the Right Mindset 86
Your First Steps Beyond This Book 86
Pitfalls to Avoid Early On 88
The Broader Vision 88
Where the Future Might Take You 89
A Final Word of Encouragement 89
Parting Thoughts 90

ABOUT CRYPTOCUBE

CryptoCube was born from experience—both the wins and the hard lessons. After being scammed and hurt in the crypto space, founder **Nadav Sananes** realised how little practical and trustworthy education was available for newcomers. The crypto world was full of noise, hype, and misinformation—but very few real tools for understanding.

Determined to change that, Nadav teamed up with **Netanel Sananes** to create a platform built on clarity, confidence, and community. Their goal: to make crypto simple, safe, and accessible to everyone.

In February 2023, **CryptoCube** was officially launched—a place where beginners can finally learn about crypto without fear or confusion and discover how this technology can empower their financial future.

Stay connected.

Every week, we share a short, no-fluff email with market insights, beginner tips, and the latest crypto updates—designed to make you smarter, not busier.

Want to join our community of learners?

Subscribe to our weekly newsletter on our website: *www.cryptocube.network*

Check our blogs for more insight updates and news in the crypto space.

Follow us on social media:

Instagram - cryptocube.network
X - @CryptoCube28
LinkedIn - CryptoCube.network
Facebook - Crypto Cube

MESSAGE FROM THE AUTHOR

Crypto Simplified was created to help everyday people—young and old alike—enter the crypto world easily and confidently. Many people hesitate to get involved in crypto due to fear, lack of knowledge, or the belief that it's too complicated. This book was designed to change that.

Inside these pages, you'll find all the essential steps and explanations needed to begin your journey with clarity. We've written this guide not only for complete beginners, but also for those already involved in crypto who want to strengthen their foundation and understanding. When learning something new, it's always wise to go back to the basics—and that's exactly what we do here.

The world of crypto is exciting, fast-evolving, and full of opportunity. Yet, many feel it's too late to start or that there's simply too much to learn. That's where **CryptoCube** comes in. Our goal is to help beginners confidently enter the crypto space, develop independence, and embrace the freedom that crypto promotes—along with the personal responsibility that comes with it.

Creating this book has been a true pleasure, and I hope it serves as a trusted guide and source of inspiration on your journey into the world of crypto.

With all my blessings,

Nadav Sananes

Founder of CryptoCube & Author of Crypto Simplified

CHAPTER 1: INTRODUCTION TO CRYPTO

Welcome to the World of Cryptocurrency

MOST PEOPLE ENCOUNTER crypto through noise—viral price charts, a friend's hot tip, a headline about a dramatic rally or crash. Behind that noise is a quiet, sturdy idea: it is possible to coordinate value on the internet without a central authority. We can transact with one another—directly and transparently—because math and code can substitute for a bank's vault and a clearinghouse's rubber stamp. If that sounds abstract now, it won't for long. By the end of this chapter, you'll understand where crypto came from, the problems it attempts to solve, and why it has already changed how millions of people store, send, and think about money.

This chapter is not a technical manual. It is a guided tour of the core motivations and the simple-but-powerful concepts that make the space coherent. We'll begin well before Bitcoin, because to understand why crypto matters, you first need to understand why money itself needed an upgrade.

The Evolution of Money: From Shells to Satoshi

Long before anyone swiped a card, typed a PIN, or scanned a QR code, people bartered. Barter was simple—grain for fish, iron for wool—but it only worked when wants matched. If the fisherman didn't want your grain today, the trade stalled. Money solved that coincidence-of-wants problem. Different societies settled on different forms: shells, salt, beads, cattle, and eventually precious metals. Metal coins made value durable, portable, and divisible; they standardized trade and unlocked more complex economies.

Paper money emerged as a promise. Early notes represented claims on gold or silver held at a bank or treasury. Over time, governments stepped away from convertibility. In the twentieth century, most nations embraced fiat currency: money not backed by metal but by law, taxation, and the credibility of the issuing state. Fiat delivered flexibility and speed, especially when paired with modern banking infrastructure. But it also centralized power. Banks maintain private ledgers and gate access to payment rails. Governments can create more currency in response to crises, shifting who bears costs and who benefits.

Computers made the system faster, not different. Your salary appears as numbers on a bank's database. Your card taps and the merchant is credited—eventually—after intermediaries reconcile. The core model remains the same: trust a chain of institutions to keep records accurate, secure, and fair. Most of the time, it works. Sometimes, it fails precisely when you need it not to—during crises, in countries with weak institutions, or in ordinary cross-border transactions that become slow and expensive because systems and rules don't interoperate.

The question that animated a generation of cryptographers and programmers was stark and simple: could the internet have native money that is scarce, programmable, borderless, and not the liability of any single institution? In 2009, an answer appeared from a pseudonym.

The Birth of Bitcoin

In the aftermath of the 2008 financial crisis—bank failures, opaque derivatives, bailouts—an author using the name Satoshi Nakamoto published a nine-page paper titled *Bitcoin: A Peer-to-Peer Electronic Cash System*. The paper described a way for strangers to agree on who owns what without asking a central bookkeeper. The trick was to make cheating more expensive than honesty and to make verification trivial for everyone else.

Bitcoin fused three ingredients:

1. **Incentives.** Participants who helped secure the network would be rewarded with newly issued coins.
2. **Cryptography.** Transactions would be signed with digital keys. Only a rightful owner could move funds.
3. **A public ledger.** Transactions would settle in batches (blocks) linked together cryptographically, and changing a past entry would break the links.

On 3 January 2009, Satoshi mined the first block (the

"genesis block") and embedded a newspaper headline about bank bailouts into its data. It was a timestamp and a thesis all at once: here is a monetary system whose rules are public and whose supply schedule—the issuance of new coins—is fixed and transparent. A hard cap of 21 million bitcoins stood in deliberate contrast to fiat's elastic supply.

In the beginning, Bitcoin's value wasn't obvious. People mined on home computers and traded coins on forums. In 2010, a developer famously bought two pizzas for 10,000 BTC—an anecdote that has become folklore. Early exchanges were fragile. Mt. Gox, which at its peak handled the majority of Bitcoin trading, collapsed in 2014 after catastrophic security failures. If Bitcoin's protocol remained intact, the lesson was brutal and clear: services around it could fail. "Not your keys, not your coins" became a core cultural axiom. The responsibility—and power—of self-custody entered the mainstream of crypto thinking.

Bitcoin survived each crisis, not because it promised no volatility or no scandals, but because its base rules held under pressure. Over time, the narrative widened. Bitcoin wasn't merely a payment rail; it was "digital gold"—portable, scarce, and natively resistant to seizure or censorship. The underlying technology, the blockchain, proved general enough that developers soon asked: what else could it enable?

What Is Cryptocurrency, Really?

A cryptocurrency is digital money that lives on a blockchain, a shared ledger maintained by many independent computers rather than a single company. No bank or government can unilaterally change this ledger. Ownership is proved with cryptographic keys: you don't request permission to move funds, you present mathematical proof that the network recognizes as valid.

Think of crypto as the internet's native value layer. It runs continuously, respects no borders, and does not close on weekends or holidays. Fees aren't for branches and back-office staff; they pay the network for security and ordering transactions. The rules are open for anyone to inspect, and software that implements those rules is widely available and auditable.

This change—from contractual control (a bank promising to honor your balance) to cryptographic control (you being able to prove your right to spend) sounds subtle; in practice, it rewires how money can be held, moved, and programmed.

How a Blockchain Works—Plainly

Imagine a notebook that anyone can read, many can write on under strict rules, and no one can erase retroactively. When you send bitcoin to a friend, your wallet creates a small message: who you're paying and how much. It signs that message with your private key—a secret known only to you. The network checks the signature and confirms you aren't trying to spend the same funds twice. Valid messages accumulate in a queue. A block producer bundles a set of them into a block. Each block includes a cryptographic fingerprint (a hash) of the previous block. Those fingerprints create links; together, the blocks form a chain.

Edit an old line, and the fingerprint changes. The links no longer match. Honest computers can instantly detect the tampering and reject your altered history. This structure makes the ledger tamper-evident. Security arises because rewriting large portions of history would require overwhelming the honest majority with enormous cost.

Different blockchains choose different rules for proposing and validating blocks, but the high-level picture is the same: a transparent, append-only ledger that many parties can verify independently.

Why Crypto Matters Now

For some, crypto is a speculative asset class. For others, it is a safety net. In places where inflation erodes salaries and savings, a scarce digital asset offers an alternative. Where capital controls and correspondent banking make cross-border transfers slow or impossible, dollar-pegged stablecoins move in minutes, often at lower cost. For freelancers in emerging markets, getting paid online without relying on an intermediary's permission can be the difference between opportunity and stagnation.

Crypto also matters because it is programmable. Developers can write smart contracts—small programs that hold funds and act automatically when conditions are met. That opens decentralized finance (DeFi): markets for swapping assets, lending and borrowing, and issuing derivatives that run transparently on-chain. It enables non-fungible tokens (NFTs): cryptographic receipts proving ownership of unique digital items. Beyond finance and culture, similar tools can secure supply-chain checkpoints, verifiable credentials, and permissionable data access.

None of this implies that crypto replaces everything. It implies that we finally have a neutral, global substrate on which new forms of value exchange, ownership, and coordination can be built.

First Steps, First Safeguards

If you're new, consider your first purchases tuition. The goal isn't to maximize returns in week one; it's to learn safely. Install a reputable wallet. Buy a tiny amount. Send a test transaction, then watch it appear on a block explorer—a website that displays the public ledger in real time. Back up your seed phrase—the 12 or 24 words that can recreate your wallet—on paper or metal and keep it offline. Never share that phrase—not with "support," not with a friend, not with anyone. Remember that on-chain transfers are final: when moving a larger sum, send a small tester first and verify it arrived. Treat any promise of "guaranteed returns" as a red flag. In crypto, skepticism is not cynicism; it is hygiene.

The Design Choices: Energy, Speed, and Trade-Offs

You will encounter debates about energy use, throughput, and fees. They reflect real trade-offs. Bitcoin uses Proof of Work (PoW), which anchors its security in physical cost (electricity and specialized hardware). That cost is a feature: attacking the network is expensive. Other blockchains use Proof of Stake (PoS), where validators lock up coins as collateral; cheating risks losing that stake. PoS consumes far less energy and can support faster throughput.

No design choice is free. Faster systems push complexity elsewhere. Lower fees today might rely on different trust assumptions. Mature projects document these choices plainly. The point for you, as a newcomer, isn't to memorize consensus mechanisms but to recognize that trade-offs exist and to prefer systems that make them explicit.

What the Ecosystem Looks Like

Think of the crypto world as layers:

- **Base layers (Layer 1s).** Independent blockchains like Bitcoin, Ethereum, Solana, and others.
- **Scaling layers (Layer 2s).** Systems that batch or compress many transactions and settle their proofs on a base layer, increasing throughput and reducing cost while inheriting base-layer security.
- **Applications.** Wallets, exchanges, lending markets, NFT platforms, payment tools—software you interact with directly.
- **Bridges and interoperability.** Tools for moving value and data between chains.

Each layer evolves. Wallets are becoming more user-friendly. Exchanges are offering clearer disclosures. Layer-2s are lowering fees. As this book progresses, you'll see how to pick suitable tools for your goals and how to operate them safely.

The Culture: Open-Source, Open Discussion

Crypto is as cultural as it is technical. Most core software is open-source: anyone can read the code, contribute, or fork it. Debates play out in public on forums, GitHub, and social media. That transparency is uncomfortable—failures and mistakes are visible—but it is also a strength. It allows rapid iteration and independent verification. It also means you will encounter hype, tribalism, and misinformation. The antidote is to seek primary sources, read documentation, and value track record over marketing.

Common Misconceptions

- **"Crypto is anonymous."** Most major blockchains are pseudonymous, not anonymous. Addresses are visible. With enough context, identities can sometimes be inferred. Privacy-preserving technologies exist, but the default is transparency.
- **"Crypto is only used by criminals."** Illicit use exists, as it does in any financial system. It is not the defining use case, and on public ledgers, illicit flows are often easier to trace than in cash-based systems.
- **"Blockchains are too slow to be useful."** Base layers prioritize security and neutrality; scale comes from layered architectures. Payments, gaming, and consumer apps increasingly run on high-throughput chains or Layer-2s.

- **"It's all speculation."** Speculation is part of any new market. But beneath price swings are working products: cross-border settlements, decentralized exchanges, credentialing tools, and micropayment systems used daily by ordinary people.

A Realistic View of Risk

Crypto is not risk-free. Prices are volatile. Smart contracts can have bugs. Exchanges can fail. Regulations can change quickly. Many tokens will not survive market cycles. These realities do not negate the value of the technology; they are reasons to adopt safe habits, use reputable tools, and size positions prudently. You can manage operational risk (how you buy, store, and move funds) even if you cannot control market risk (prices rising or falling). This book will teach both.

The Broader Vision

Satoshi wrote that the root problem with conventional currency is all the trust required to make it work. Crypto reduces the need for blind trust by replacing it with transparent rules that anyone can verify. It does not abolish institutions or laws; it offers an alternative foundation—neutral, open, and global by default—upon which institutions can build and compete. The first internet made information cheap to move. This one makes value programmable. The claim is ambitious; the evidence is practical, visible in public ledgers and live applications rather than hidden in private databases.

Where We Go Next

In the chapters ahead, we will make these ideas concrete. You will learn what a wallet really is and how to use one with confidence. You will understand how transactions move, what fees you are paying and why, and how different blockchains prioritize security, speed, and cost. You will meet the major cryptocurrencies and see the trade-offs they embody. You will choose tools—wallets, exchanges, and apps—that match your goals. You will learn the mechanics of buying and selling, the mindsets behind trading and holding, and, crucially, how to protect what you own.

For now, remember this: crypto is not a shortcut to riches, nor is it a passing fad. It is a new set of building blocks for money and markets. Treat your first steps with respect. Go slowly. Verify rather than assume. Ask how things work. And enjoy the feeling that accompanies learning something genuinely new—because that feeling is the surest sign you're early to a technology that matters.

CHAPTER 2: CRYPTO BASICS

NOW THAT YOU'VE been introduced to the idea of cryptocurrency and its origins, it's time to get a little more practical. This chapter will serve as your foundation for understanding the basic building blocks of the crypto world. By the time you finish, you'll know what makes crypto different from traditional money, how wallets work, what a transaction looks like, why blockchains come in different forms, and how people actually use crypto in everyday life. Think of this chapter as equipping you with the essential toolkit you'll need before moving into more advanced concepts.

What Exactly Is Crypto?

Cryptocurrency, at its simplest, is digital money. But unlike the digital numbers you see when you log in to your online banking account, crypto is not controlled by a bank, government, or single institution. It is decentralized money that exists on a global computer network called the blockchain.

To understand how unique this is, let's compare it with traditional money. When you swipe your debit card at a store, the bank updates its internal ledger to say that some money has left your account and entered the merchant's account. All of this happens behind the scenes, and you have to trust the bank to be accurate and honest. With cryptocurrency, however, the ledger is public, shared across thousands of computers, and updated in a way that doesn't require trust in any person or institution.

There are three main characteristics that make cryptocurrency what it is: it's digital, decentralized, and peer-to-peer. Being digital means it has no physical form—it exists entirely as code. Being decentralized means there isn't a single central bank or government running the system. And being peer-to-peer means that transactions happen directly between people, without the need to go through banks, payment processors, or other intermediaries.

This design is what makes cryptocurrency so powerful. Instead of relying on old systems built around paperwork, intermediaries, and trust in institutions, crypto allows value to move directly between people, instantly and globally.

Understanding Crypto Wallets

Before you can buy, send, or receive cryptocurrency, you need a place to store it. This is where wallets come in. A crypto wallet isn't a physical container—it's more like a digital tool that interacts with the blockchain on your behalf. You can think of it as your personal interface with the crypto world.

There are two main types of wallets: hot wallets and cold wallets.

Hot wallets are connected to the internet. They're usually mobile apps or browser extensions, such as MetaMask, Trust Wallet, or Phantom. Because they are online, they're very convenient—you can quickly send or receive crypto anytime. However, the fact that they're online makes them more vulnerable to hacking.

Cold wallets, on the other hand, are offline storage solutions. These are physical devices like hardware wallets (Ledger, Trezor, ColdCard) or even paper wallets that store your keys without touching the internet. They are extremely secure but less convenient for quick transactions. Most experienced users will keep their long-term holdings in a cold wallet and only small amounts in hot wallets for daily use.

What really defines a wallet is the pair of cryptographic keys it manages for you: a **public key** and a **private key**. The public key is like your bank account number—you can share it freely with anyone who wants to send you crypto. The private key is like the password to your account, but even more sensitive. Whoever holds the private key controls the funds in that wallet. This is why one of the most important rules in crypto is simple: never share your private key or seed phrase with anyone.

If you lose your private key or seed phrase, you lose access to your funds forever. There's no "forgot password" button or customer support number to call. This level of personal responsibility is part of what makes crypto empowering—but it can also be intimidating for beginners. Don't worry, though. With the right practices, securing your wallet is straightforward, and we'll go deeper into security later in the book.

How Transactions Work

Now that you know about wallets, let's look at what happens when you actually send or receive cryptocurrency.

Imagine that Alice wants to send one Bitcoin to Bob. She opens her wallet app, enters Bob's public address, and confirms the transaction. Behind the scenes, her wallet signs the transaction using her private key, proving that she is the rightful owner of the Bitcoin she's sending. The transaction is then broadcast to the entire Bitcoin network.

The network of computers running Bitcoin—called nodes—checks to make sure Alice actually has one Bitcoin to send and that she isn't trying to spend the same coin twice. Once verified, the transaction is placed into a pool of pending transactions.

From here, miners (or validators, depending on the blockchain) take over. They bundle Alice's transaction together with others into a block and add it to the blockchain. Once this happens, the Bitcoin officially belongs to Bob, and he can see it in his wallet.

This system might sound complicated, but the beauty of it is that you don't need to understand all the technical details every time you make a transaction. Just like you don't need to know the mechanics of how a bank clears a check, you don't need to know exactly how miners validate transactions. What you do need to know is that the system is designed to be secure, transparent, and trustless.

Mining and Validation

To better understand why crypto transactions are secure, it's worth looking briefly at how mining—or in newer blockchains, validation—works.

Bitcoin introduced the idea of **Proof of Work (PoW)**. In this system, miners compete to solve complex mathematical puzzles. The first miner to solve the puzzle gets to add a new block of transactions to the blockchain and is rewarded with newly created Bitcoin plus transaction fees. This process is energy-intensive but extremely secure, as it would require an enormous amount of computing power to cheat the system.

Newer blockchains, such as Ethereum after its 2022 transition, use **Proof of Stake (PoS)** instead. In PoS, validators are chosen to add new blocks based on how many coins they hold and are willing to "stake" as collateral. This system is far more energy-efficient than mining and allows for faster transactions. However, it has more influence on those who hold larger amounts of the cryptocurrency.

Both systems—Proof of Work and Proof of Stake—are forms of consensus mechanisms. Their job is to make sure everyone in the network agrees on the state of the blockchain without relying on a central authority.

Public vs. Private Blockchains

Not all blockchains are the same. Some, like Bitcoin and Ethereum, are public blockchains, meaning anyone can join the network, send transactions, or even help validate blocks. These are transparent and open systems designed for maximum decentralization.

Private blockchains, by contrast, are restricted networks. They are often used by businesses or governments for internal purposes, such as supply chain management or secure record-keeping. These blockchains sacrifice decentralization for speed, efficiency, and privacy.

Understanding this distinction helps you see how blockchain technology can be applied far beyond cryptocurrency itself.

A Deeper Look at Ethereum

Although we touched on Ethereum earlier, it's worth going a little deeper here, because Ethereum introduces a concept that completely changed the crypto world: smart contracts.

A smart contract is simply code that runs on the blockchain. It can automatically execute actions when certain conditions are met, without the need for a middleman. For example, a smart contract can be programmed to release payment to a freelancer only after they deliver work, or to refund investors if a project doesn't meet its funding goal.

This innovation turned Ethereum into more than just a digital currency. It became a programmable platform on which developers could build decentralized applications (dApps). These applications can do everything from facilitating decentralized finance (DeFi) services like lending and borrowing, to powering blockchain-based games, to creating marketplaces for NFTs (non-fungible tokens).

In other words, while Bitcoin proved that decentralized money was possible, Ethereum proved that entire decentralized economies could exist.

Everyday Uses of Crypto

So far, you've learned how crypto works under the hood. But what can you actually do with it in real life?

One of the most obvious uses is as a medium of exchange. Increasingly, businesses accept Bitcoin, Ethereum, or stablecoins as payment. Some online retailers, coffee shops, and even airlines have begun to take crypto directly. In countries with unstable currencies, like Venezuela or Zimbabwe, people use stablecoins pegged to the US dollar as a more reliable way to store value and make payments.

Another common use is sending money across borders. Traditional remittances can take days and involve high fees. With crypto, someone can send money internationally in minutes, often at a fraction of the cost. For migrant workers, sending money home to family is life-changing.

Crypto is also widely used for investing. Many people buy Bitcoin or Ethereum as a long-term store of value, often comparing Bitcoin to "digital gold." Others speculate on altcoins, hoping to profit from short-term price movements.

And then there's the world of DeFi, where people can earn interest, borrow funds, or trade assets—all without needing a bank. DeFi protocols are like automated financial services running on smart contracts, open to anyone with a smartphone and internet connection.

The Rise of Altcoins

While Bitcoin and Ethereum dominate the conversation, they are far from the only cryptocurrencies out there. Today, there are thousands of altcoins (any cryptocurrency other than

Bitcoin). Some, like Litecoin or Ripple (XRP), were designed as improvements or alternatives to Bitcoin. Others, like Solana or Cardano, focus on solving specific technical challenges such as scalability or energy efficiency.

Each cryptocurrency has its own purpose and vision, but many will fade away over time. For beginners, the important thing is to recognize that not all coins are created equal. Some are serious projects with strong teams and real-world use cases, while others are little more than hype-driven experiments. Part of becoming knowledgeable in crypto is learning how to tell the difference, which we'll cover in later chapters.

Building Toward the Next Step

At this point, you should have a solid grasp of the basics. You understand what makes cryptocurrency unique, how wallets and transactions work, the role of miners and validators, the difference between public and private blockchains, and some of the ways people actually use crypto in their daily lives.

This foundation is critical because everything else you'll learn in this book builds on it. In the next chapter, we'll dive deeper into the **fundamentals**—concepts like decentralization, cryptography, consensus mechanisms, and tokenomics. These are the principles that explain why crypto works the way it does and why it has the potential to reshape the world of finance and beyond.

CHAPTER 3: FUNDAMENTALS

WELCOME to one of the most important stages of your crypto journey: understanding the fundamentals. While the previous chapters introduced you to what cryptocurrency is and how to get started, this chapter goes deeper. Here, we'll unpack the principles that make cryptocurrency work, the economic forces behind it, the technologies that secure it, and the systems that ensure people around the world can agree on the same version of truth without relying on a bank, government, or corporation.

Grasping these fundamentals is essential because they provide the "why" behind everything else. Without this layer of understanding, you might see cryptocurrency as just a speculative asset or a technological fad. But once you understand the principles of decentralization, cryptography, consensus, and tokenomics, you'll begin to see why crypto represents a profound shift in how humans organize trust and exchange value.

Let's explore these building blocks.

Decentralization: Power Spread Out

At the core of every cryptocurrency is **decentralization**. This word is used a lot, but what does it really mean?

Decentralization means that no single authority is in charge. In traditional systems, whether it's your bank, your government, or a social media platform, one entity holds ultimate control. They can decide who participates, censor or block access and change the rules if they see fit.

Cryptocurrency flips this model on its head. Instead of one central authority maintaining the system, thousands of independent computers, called nodes, collectively run the network. These nodes all have a copy of the same ledger and work together to validate transactions. No one node has more control than the others, and the system continues to function even if many nodes go offline.

This has several implications:

- **Resilience.** Because there is no central server, the system can't be shut down by simply targeting one location. To "turn off" Bitcoin, for example, you would need to simultaneously disable thousands of computers across nearly every country in the world.
- **Censorship resistance.** A decentralized system cannot easily prevent a user from participating. As long as you have internet access and a wallet, you can send and receive transactions, regardless of who you are or where you live.
- **Democratization of trust.** Instead of trusting an authority, participants trust the system itself—the

math, the code, and the collective verification of all nodes.

Think of decentralization like the difference between a monarchy and a democracy. In a monarchy, one ruler makes the decisions. In a democracy, power is distributed, and no single individual can easily impose their will. In cryptocurrency, decentralization means the system belongs to everyone, not just to a few powerful players.

Cryptography: The Science of Security

The second pillar of cryptocurrency is **cryptography**, the field of mathematics that secures information. Without cryptography, decentralization wouldn't work—people would cheat, transactions could be altered, and trust would collapse.

Cryptography solves these problems by making it practically impossible to alter records or impersonate others.

Hash Functions

One of the most important cryptographic tools used in crypto is the **hash function**. A hash takes an input of any size (like a transaction record) and produces a fixed-length output of numbers and letters. What's fascinating about a hash is that even the smallest change in input produces a completely different output.

For example, if you hash the sentence "I sent one Bitcoin," you might get a string of characters like 4c2f.... If you change it to "I sent two Bitcoin," the output is entirely different.

This is crucial for blockchains because hashes make

records tamper-evident. Each block contains the hash of the previous block. If someone tries to change even a single transaction in a past block, the hash will no longer match, and the network will immediately reject it.

Public and Private Keys

Another critical use of cryptography is in the generation of keys. Every crypto wallet contains two keys: a public key and a private key.

- The **public key** acts like your address. You can share it with anyone who wants to send you funds.
- The **private key** is your secret. It's used to sign transactions, proving you are the rightful owner of the funds.

The magic here is that cryptography allows you to share your public key freely without ever revealing your private key. This is what enables secure peer-to-peer transactions without intermediaries.

Digital Signatures

When you send crypto, your wallet uses your private key to create a digital signature. This signature proves two things: that you are the owner of the funds being sent, and that the transaction has not been altered in transit. Every node in the network can verify your signature using your public key, but they cannot reverse-engineer your private key from it.

This combination of hashes, keys, and signatures creates the backbone of blockchain security.

Supply, Demand, and Scarcity

Beyond technology, cryptocurrencies also operate according to economic fundamentals—chief among them are supply and demand. Unlike traditional currencies, which governments can print at will, many cryptocurrencies have fixed or predictable supplies. This scarcity is what gives them value.

Take **Bitcoin** as the classic example. There will only ever be 21 million Bitcoins programmed into the code itself. This hard cap is part of Bitcoin's appeal, especially in a world where governments frequently print more money, devaluing the existing supply through inflation.

Ethereum, on the other hand, does not have a strict cap. Instead, its supply is managed through mechanisms like "burning," where a portion of transaction fees is permanently removed from circulation. This creates a dynamic balance between new issuance and destruction, sometimes making Ethereum deflationary.

Scarcity matters because it influences how people perceive value. Just like gold is precious because it is rare and difficult to mine, Bitcoin is valuable because it is scarce and difficult to produce. The more people demand it while supply remains fixed, the higher its price tends to rise.

Consensus Mechanisms: Reaching Agreement Without Trust

If decentralization spreads out control, and cryptography secures the system, then consensus mechanisms are the rules that allow thousands of independent nodes to agree on the same version of truth.

In centralized systems, consensus is easy—the central authority decides. But in decentralized systems, where no single authority is in charge, there needs to be a way for everyone to agree on which transactions are valid. That's what consensus mechanisms provide.

Proof of Work (PoW)

Bitcoin's consensus mechanism is Proof of Work. In this system, miners use powerful computers to solve mathematical puzzles. Solving the puzzle proves they've done the "work" required to validate a block. The winning miner adds the block to the blockchain and is rewarded with new Bitcoin and transaction fees.

PoW is highly secure because altering the blockchain would require redoing all the work for every block, which is computationally infeasible. The drawback is that it consumes a lot of energy.

Proof of Stake (PoS)

Ethereum, after its 2022 upgrade known as "The Merge," moved to Proof of Stake. Here, validators are chosen to create blocks based on how many coins they hold and are willing to "stake" as collateral. If they act dishonestly, they lose their stake.

PoS is far more energy-efficient than PoW and allows for faster transaction times. The trade-off is that it gives greater influence to wealthier participants, since those with larger stakes are more likely to be chosen as validators.

Other Models

There are also other consensus models worth noting:

- **Delegated Proof of Stake (DPoS).** Used by blockchains like EOS and TRON, this system allows token holders to vote for a small group of delegates who validate transactions on their behalf. It's faster and more efficient, but it can lead to centralization.
- **Proof of Authority (PoA).** Often used in private blockchains, where a small number of trusted entities validate transactions. This model prioritizes speed and efficiency over decentralization.

Each system has its strengths and weaknesses, and different blockchains choose based on their goals.

Ethereum's Merge: A Case Study

Ethereum's transition from Proof of Work to Proof of Stake, known as **The Merge**, illustrates how consensus mechanisms evolve.

This shift reduced Ethereum's energy consumption by more than 99%, addressing one of the biggest criticisms of blockchains. It also paved the way for future scalability improvements, allowing Ethereum to process more transactions at lower costs.

The Merge demonstrated that blockchains are not static; they can upgrade and adapt to meet new challenges. It was one of the most significant technological events in crypto history, showing the industry's willingness to innovate and prioritize sustainability.

Tokenomics: The Economics of Tokens

To truly understand cryptocurrencies, you need to understand **tokenomics**, or the economic systems that give tokens their value. Tokenomics looks at how tokens are created, distributed, and used within a blockchain ecosystem.

Supply

The first consideration is supply. A token's circulating supply is how many tokens are currently in the market, while the total supply is the maximum number that can ever exist. Scarcity can drive value, as we saw with Bitcoin's 21 million cap.

Utility

The second consideration is utility—what can you actually do with the token? Some tokens serve as digital money, others power decentralized applications, and still others grant voting rights in decentralized governance systems.

For example:

- Bitcoin's utility is as a store of value and medium of exchange.
- Ethereum's utility is as "gas" to pay for transactions and smart contracts.
- Governance tokens like UNI (from Uniswap) give holders voting power over protocol decisions.

INCENTIVES

Tokenomics also includes incentive structures. Miners, validators, and users are all motivated by rewards built into the system. If a blockchain is designed well, these incentives encourage honest behavior and network participation.

Risks and Challenges

While crypto is full of potential, it's not without risks. Understanding these challenges is part of grasping the fundamentals.

VOLATILITY

Cryptocurrency prices can rise and fall dramatically within hours. This volatility creates opportunities for traders but can be unnerving for beginners.

. . .

Scams and Hacks

Because crypto is decentralized and irreversible, it attracts scammers. From fake projects to phishing attacks, there are many ways for the careless to lose funds. We'll cover security in detail later in the book.

Regulation

Governments are still figuring out how to regulate cryptocurrency. Some countries embrace it, others ban it, and many are undecided. Regulatory uncertainty can impact prices and adoption.

Building Up to the Next Chapter

At this point, you've peeled back the curtain on what makes cryptocurrency work. You've seen how decentralization spreads power, how cryptography secures the system, how consensus keeps everyone aligned, and how tokenomics shapes value.

These fundamentals are the invisible machinery behind every transaction you'll ever make in the crypto world. Without them, cryptocurrency would be no different from any other form of digital money controlled by banks or corporations.

In the next chapter, we'll focus entirely on the technology that powers it all: the blockchain itself. You'll learn why blockchain is considered revolutionary, how it goes beyond crypto into industries like supply chains and healthcare, and why many experts believe it could become as transformative as the internet.

CHAPTER 4: WHY BLOCKCHAIN IS SO AWESOME

The Hidden Engine Behind Cryptocurrency

EVERY CAR NEEDS AN ENGINE. Every house needs a foundation. And every cryptocurrency needs a blockchain. Without the blockchain, Bitcoin would just be another digital file you could copy endlessly, like a song or a photo. Ethereum would just be another database. Solana, Cardano, and the rest of the crypto universe would not exist.

The blockchain is the invisible infrastructure that makes everything else possible. It ensures that transactions are valid, prevents double-spending, and creates a public, tamper-proof history of events. More than that, it has opened a door to innovations far beyond currency—into finance, identity, logistics, art, and even governance.

In this chapter, we'll unpack why blockchain matters, how it works at a deeper level, where it's already proving useful, and why it's considered one of the most powerful technological inventions of the 21st century.

A Story of Shared Truth

Imagine a group of friends who decide to play a game together. They write down every move in a shared notebook. But instead of leaving the notebook with one person, each friend has their own identical copy. Every time a move is made, they all write it down at the same time.

Now imagine someone tries to cheat—maybe they try to erase their last move. The moment they do, their notebook is out of sync with everyone else's. The group immediately spots the difference, rejects the altered version, and continues using the copies that match.

That's the essence of blockchain: a shared history that everyone maintains and no one can secretly alter. It's a digital "notebook" distributed across thousands of computers around the world.

This simple but powerful idea—maintaining consensus without a central authority—is what makes blockchain so revolutionary.

How a Blockchain Actually Works

At its core, a blockchain is just a ledger: a record of transactions. But unlike a bank ledger stored on one company's servers, this ledger is:

- **Public.** Anyone can view it, anytime, from anywhere.
- **Distributed.** Copies of the ledger exist on thousands of independent nodes.

- **Immutable.** Once information is recorded and confirmed, it cannot easily be changed.

Blocks and Chains

Transactions are grouped together into "blocks." Each block contains:

- A list of valid transactions.
- A timestamp.
- A reference (hash) to the previous block.

This last piece is critical. By linking each block to the one before it, the blockchain forms an unbroken chain of history. If someone tries to change an old block, its hash changes, breaking the link and alerting the entire network.

Consensus and Security

Blockchains also rely on **consensus mechanisms** (discussed in the last chapter) to decide which new block is added next. Whether through Proof of Work, Proof of Stake, or another model, the process ensures that the majority of nodes agree on the true history.

The result is a system that doesn't require blind trust in one authority. Instead, it relies on open rules, cryptography, and the economic incentives of participants.

Why Blockchain Is a Big Deal

If all this sounds technical, let's make it practical: why does blockchain matter? Why do people call it "the next internet"?

1. Transparency and Trust

Every transaction is recorded publicly. Anyone can verify what happened, when it happened, and how much was involved. This transparency builds trust without the need for intermediaries. In traditional finance, you trust banks and auditors to keep honest books. On a blockchain, the ledger itself is the book, open to all.

2. Security and Tamper Resistance

Because blocks are linked by hashes and secured by consensus, altering history is extremely difficult. To rewrite a blockchain, an attacker would need to control most of the network's power, a task that grows nearly impossible as the network scales. This makes blockchains highly resistant to tampering, fraud, and censorship.

3. Global Accessibility

Anyone with internet access can join. You don't need a bank account, a credit score, or government approval. This "permissionless" nature is why crypto has grown so quickly in developing nations, where access to traditional financial infrastructure is limited.

4. Efficiency Through Automation

Smart contracts—programs that run on blockchains—can automate transactions without intermediaries. For example, instead of using a bank to escrow funds in a property deal, you can use a smart contract that automatically releases payment when both sides fulfill the agreed conditions. Less paperwork, less delay, and fewer middlemen.

5. Programmability

Unlike traditional ledgers, blockchains are programmable. Ethereum pioneered this idea with smart contracts, turning the ledger into a global computer. Developers can build decentralized apps (dApps) for trading, lending, gaming, identity, and more.

Beyond Money: Real-World Use Cases

Blockchain began with Bitcoin as digital cash, but its applications extend far beyond finance. Here are some of the most impactful areas where blockchain is already proving useful:

Supply Chains

From food to fashion, supply chains involve multiple players across borders. Traditionally, this creates opacity—was the coffee really fair-trade? Was the diamond really conflict-free? Blockchain allows all participants to log each step, creating a transparent record from origin to shelf. Companies like Walmart have tested blockchain for tracking produce to improve recall efficiency.

Healthcare

Medical records are often fragmented across hospitals, labs, and clinics. Blockchain can give patients ownership of their records while allowing doctors or insurers to access them securely. It can also verify the authenticity of pharmaceuticals, reducing counterfeit risks.

Identity and Credentials

Billions of people lack formal identification, making it hard to access banking, education, or healthcare. Blockchain-based IDs can provide secure, portable identity systems. Similarly, educational institutions can issue tamper-proof diplomas and certificates on-chain.

Digital Ownership (NFTs)

Non-Fungible Tokens (NFTs) exploded into the mainstream as digital art collectibles, but their potential goes further. NFTs can represent ownership of music, in-game assets, domain names, or even tickets. The blockchain proves authenticity and ownership, preventing duplication or fraud.

Governance and Voting

Some projects use blockchain for decentralized governance. Token holders can vote on protocol upgrades or treasury decisions, with results transparently recorded on-chain. Governments have also experimented with blockchain-based voting to increase trust in elections.

Success Stories and Experiments

- **Estonia.** This small European country uses blockchain-inspired infrastructure to secure healthcare, judicial, and property records. It's one of the best examples of blockchain enhancing government services.
- **El Salvador.** In 2021, El Salvador became the first nation to adopt Bitcoin as legal tender, aiming to reduce remittance costs for citizens abroad. The experiment is ongoing and controversial, but it illustrates how nations are testing blockchain at scale.
- **DeFi Explosion.** Decentralized finance (DeFi) protocols like Aave, Compound, and Uniswap have created open lending and trading markets with billions of dollars locked in smart contracts, all without traditional banks.

These examples show that blockchain is no longer just a theory. It's already reshaping industries, even if mainstream adoption is uneven.

Challenges and Criticisms

Of course, blockchain isn't perfect. For every innovation, there are challenges that skeptics rightly point out.

Scalability

Most blockchains can't handle as many transactions per second as centralized systems like Visa. Solutions like **Layer-2 networks** (e.g., Lightning Network for Bitcoin, rollups for Ethereum) aim to fix this by processing transactions off-chain and settling them later.

Energy Use

Proof of Work blockchains like Bitcoin consume significant energy. Supporters argue this secures the network and incentivizes renewable energy use, while critics call it wasteful. Proof of Stake and other consensus models reduce this issue dramatically.

Regulation

Governments worry about money laundering, consumer protection, and financial stability. Some countries have embraced blockchain; others have banned aspects of it. Clear, balanced regulation remains a global challenge.

User Experience

Crypto is still not as simple as swiping a credit card. Managing private keys, seed phrases, and wallets can be intimidating. Better interfaces are needed before billions of people adopt blockchain-based systems seamlessly.

The Big Picture: The Internet of Value

The internet we know today has made information abundant, fast, and global. Blockchain does the same for value. It allows money, assets, and agreements to move as freely as emails or videos.

This is why blockchain is often called the **Internet of Value**. It transforms money into a software primitive, ownership into a transferable digital record, and trust into code that anyone can verify.

Just as email replaced letters and search engines replaced phone books, blockchain has the potential to replace or radically improve many of the systems we rely on for commerce, identity, and coordination.

Closing Thoughts

Blockchain is not just "hype" or a buzzword. It's a fundamental innovation in how humans record and share truth. It takes power away from central authorities and distributes it across open networks. It creates transparent systems where anyone can verify the rules for themselves. And it unlocks new ways of coordinating finance, trade, and ownership on a global scale.

Yes, challenges remain. But even with its current limitations, blockchain is already reshaping industries and inspiring experiments across the globe. As adoption grows and technology matures, its role will only expand.

In the next chapter, we'll shift from the engine to the vehicles it powers: the major cryptocurrencies themselves. From

Bitcoin and Ethereum to Solana, Cardano, and beyond, you'll meet the projects that define the crypto landscape today, understand their differences, and see how each fits into the broader story of digital value.

CHAPTER 5: THE MAIN CRYPTOCURRENCIES

Meeting the Giants of the Crypto World

IF BLOCKCHAIN IS THE ENGINE, cryptocurrencies are the vehicles that run on it. Some are rugged, built for endurance; others are sleek, optimized for speed or flexibility. Together, they form a diverse ecosystem that reflects the many visions for how digital value can and should work.

Understanding the major cryptocurrencies is like learning the languages of different countries. Each coin speaks to its community's priorities—scarcity, speed, programmability, interoperability—and each has carved out its own place in the market. In this chapter, we'll trace the origins of the most important coins, examine what makes them unique, and explore the roles they play today.

We'll begin with the early pioneers—Bitcoin, Litecoin, Namecoin, Peercoin, and XRP—that established the first foundations. Then we'll move to the dominant players of today: Ethereum, BNB Chain, Cardano, Solana, and Polkadot.

Bitcoin (BTC): Scarcity with a Spine

Bitcoin is the cornerstone of the entire cryptocurrency movement. Born in 2009 from Satoshi Nakamoto's whitepaper, it introduced the world to a new idea: money that is not issued by governments, not controlled by banks, and not reliant on trust in middlemen.

What makes Bitcoin radical is its rules. Only 21 million will ever exist. New coins enter circulation at a predictable pace, halving every four years, until eventually no new Bitcoin is mined. This supply schedule contrasts starkly with fiat currencies, where central banks can print at will. In a world of inflationary pressures, Bitcoin stands as digital gold: scarce, portable, divisible, and resistant to censorship.

Early on, Bitcoin was used as peer-to-peer cash. Famously, in 2010, a programmer named Laszlo Hanyecz bought two pizzas for 10,000 BTC—worth billions of dollars at today's prices. Over time, however, its narrative shifted. Rising transaction fees and slower confirmation times made it less practical for everyday payments, but its durability and neutrality made it an ideal store of value.

Today, Bitcoin is held by individuals, institutions, and even nations. El Salvador adopted it as legal tender in 2021. Major companies add it to their balance sheets as a hedge against monetary debasement. And millions of people around the world use it as a lifeline where banking access is limited or unstable.

Technological layers expand Bitcoin's use cases. The Lightning Network allows instant, low-fee payments, keeping Bitcoin's core secure while enabling fast transactions off-chain. Experiments like Ordinals (inscribing data or NFTs onto Bitcoin) show that even a "conservative" protocol continues to evolve.

Bitcoin's genius lies in its simplicity: a transparent, incorruptible ledger and a monetary policy that has never wavered. It remains the benchmark against which all other cryptocurrencies are measured.

Litecoin (LTC): The Silver to Bitcoin's Gold

Created in 2011 by Charlie Lee, a former Google engineer, Litecoin set out to be a lighter, faster version of Bitcoin. Its block time is 2.5 minutes (compared to Bitcoin's 10), meaning transactions confirm more quickly. It also uses a different hashing algorithm, Scrypt, which was designed to make mining more accessible to ordinary computers (though specialized hardware eventually caught up).

Litecoin has often been called the "silver to Bitcoin's gold." It doesn't try to reinvent the wheel: instead, it offers familiarity with a few tweaks. Importantly, Litecoin has served as a testing ground for upgrades. Segregated Witness (SegWit), a scaling improvement later adopted by Bitcoin, was implemented on Litecoin first. Similarly, Litecoin was among the first to experiment with the Lightning Network.

Its value today is less about innovation and more about endurance. Litecoin has survived countless market cycles, exchange collapses, and technological shifts. While newer, flashier projects have come and gone, Litecoin remains one of the most widely supported and liquid cryptocurrencies, trusted by many as a straightforward, low-cost option for transfers.

Namecoin (NMC): The First Experiment Beyond Money

Namecoin, launched in 2011, was the first cryptocurrency to push blockchain beyond payments. Its creators envisioned a decentralized domain name system (DNS). Instead of registering your website through centralized providers like ICANN, you could register a ".bit" domain on Namecoin's blockchain.

This was an early attempt at digital sovereignty: owning your online identity without reliance on centralized authorities. In practice, adoption was limited. Few browsers natively support ".bit" domains, and managing them proved cumbersome. Still, the idea was revolutionary. It showed that blockchains could secure not just financial transactions but other kinds of valuable records.

Today, Namecoin is mostly a historical artifact, but its influence is clear. Projects working on decentralized identity and naming systems—like Ethereum Name Service (ENS)—stand on Namecoin's shoulders. It was a glimpse of blockchain's potential as a registry of truth, not just a ledger of money.

Peercoin (PPC): Early Steps Toward Sustainability

Peercoin, launched in 2012 by developers Sunny King and Scott Nadal, introduced a concept that has since become central to the industry: Proof of Stake (PoS).

At the time, Bitcoin's Proof of Work was already drawing criticism for its energy use. Peercoin's creators sought a greener alternative. Their solution was hybrid: new blocks could be produced both through mining (Proof of Work) and through staking, where coin holders lock up funds and are chosen to validate transactions.

Peercoin didn't achieve mass adoption, but it made history as the first blockchain to implement Proof of Stake. That innovation paved the way for later giants like Ethereum, which in 2022 transitioned fully to PoS, reducing its energy consumption by over 99%.

Peercoin's story underscores an important lesson: not every pioneer thrives long-term, but even experiments that fade can influence the path of an entire industry.

XRP Ledger (XRP): Speeding Up the Plumbing of Finance

Launched in 2012 by a group of developers including Jed McCaleb, Arthur Britto, and David Schwartz, the XRP Ledger aimed to solve a specific problem: slow and expensive international money transfers.

In traditional finance, cross-border payments pass through a maze of correspondent banks, each taking fees and adding delays. The XRP Ledger offered an alternative: near-instant settlement with very low fees. Ripple Labs, the company associated with the project, partnered with financial institutions to test using XRP as a "bridge currency" for moving value between different fiat systems.

The XRP Ledger doesn't rely on mining. Instead, it uses a unique consensus protocol where validators agree on which transactions are valid. This allows for high speed (thousands of transactions per second) and efficiency.

XRP has also faced controversy. The U.S. Securities and Exchange Commission (SEC) sued Ripple Labs in 2020, arguing XRP was sold as an unregistered security. After years of litigation, parts of the case remain unresolved, but in 2023, a court ruled that XRP itself is not inherently a security.

Despite the legal battles, XRP remains one of the most widely traded cryptocurrencies. For users and institutions seeking speed and predictability in cross-border settlement, the XRP Ledger continues to provide a unique option in the crypto landscape.

Ethereum (ETH): The World Computer

Bitcoin proved that decentralized money was possible. Ethereum, launched in 2015 by Vitalik Buterin and a team of developers, proved that decentralized applications were possible.

Ethereum's big innovation was the **smart contract**: self-executing code that runs on the blockchain. Instead of just recording balances, Ethereum could enforce conditions. This transformed blockchain from a ledger into a global computer.

The implications were enormous. Decentralized Finance (DeFi) was born, enabling lending, borrowing, and trading without banks. Non-Fungible Tokens (NFTs) exploded into art, gaming, and entertainment. Decentralized Autonomous Organizations (DAOs) emerged as new forms of governance.

Ethereum itself has evolved significantly. Originally running on Proof of Work, it transitioned to Proof of Stake in 2022 through "The Merge," a technical achievement likened to swapping a jet engine mid-flight. This reduced its energy use by more than 99% and set the stage for scaling through

Layer-2 solutions, which bundle transactions and post proofs back to Ethereum.

Ethereum is sometimes criticized for high gas fees during peak demand, but it remains the hub of innovation in crypto. Its flexibility, developer community, and first-mover advantage make it the backbone of Web3. If Bitcoin is digital gold, Ethereum is digital infrastructure.

BNB Chain (BNB): From Exchange Token to Ecosystem Powerhouse

BNB began in 2017 as Binance Coin, a token used to reduce fees on Binance, the world's largest cryptocurrency exchange. Over time, it grew into much more.

Binance launched its own blockchain, now called BNB Chain, which supports smart contracts and decentralized applications. Unlike Ethereum, BNB Chain is optimized for high throughput and low fees. This made it attractive for developers who wanted fast, inexpensive transactions and access to Binance's enormous user base.

BNB's utility has expanded: it powers transaction fees on BNB Chain, is used in DeFi apps, and is periodically burned by Binance to reduce supply. Despite criticism that the network is more centralized (a relatively small number of validators control block production), BNB Chain has remained one of the busiest blockchains in terms of daily transactions.

Regulators worldwide keep a close eye on Binance, and by extension, BNB. But for millions of users, BNB Chain offers a practical, accessible way to engage with crypto at lower costs than Ethereum.

Cardano (ADA): Science Meets Blockchain

Founded by Ethereum co-founder Charles Hoskinson in 2017, Cardano took a different approach: rigorous academic research and peer-reviewed development. Its consensus protocol, Ouroboros, is one of the first Proof of Stake mechanisms formally proven to be secure.

Cardano emphasizes scalability, sustainability, and security. Its roadmap has rolled out in carefully staged phases: Byron (foundation), Shelley (decentralization), Goguen (smart contracts), and beyond. Critics argue this cautious approach slows adoption. Supporters argue it ensures reliability and avoids the "move fast and break things" pitfalls that have plagued other projects.

Cardano's smart contract capabilities, added in 2021, opened the door for DeFi and NFT activity on its chain. It has also been involved in real-world projects, particularly in emerging markets—such as blockchain-based identity systems for students in Ethiopia.

While Cardano doesn't dominate transaction volume the way Ethereum or Solana does, its methodical development and passionate community give it a distinctive place in the ecosystem. It represents the "research-first" school of blockchain design.

Solana (SOL): The Speed Demon

Launched in 2020 by former Qualcomm engineer Anatoly Yakovenko, Solana set out to solve one of blockchain's biggest challenges: scalability. Its key innovation is Proof of History, a cryptographic clock that allows validators to agree on transaction order quickly. Combined with Proof of Stake, this design enables extremely fast throughput—tens of thousands of transactions per second—with very low fees.

Solana quickly became a favorite for applications that demand speed: high-frequency trading, gaming, and NFT marketplaces. Collections like Degenerate Apes and projects like Magic Eden flourished in Solana's ecosystem.

However, speed came with growing pains. In its early years, Solana experienced several network outages, leading critics to question its reliability. Developers responded by improving client diversity, validator infrastructure, and resilience.

Despite the hiccups, Solana has retained strong momentum. Its cheap, fast transactions make it attractive to builders and users alike, and its ecosystem continues to expand rapidly. Solana is often described as "Ethereum's rival," but its focus on performance positions it differently: not as a replacement, but as an alternative for web-scale applications.

Polkadot (DOT): The Multichain Vision

Polkadot, launched in 2020 by Ethereum co-founder Gavin Wood, takes a different approach to blockchain's scalability challenge. Instead of one chain trying to do everything, Polkadot is a **multichain network**.

Its architecture is built around a central Relay Chain that provides security and coordination. Attached to it are multiple parachains—specialized blockchains optimized for particular tasks, such as privacy, gaming, or DeFi. These parachains can communicate and share information, solving one of blockchain's biggest problems: interoperability.

Polkadot's vision is a web of blockchains that work together seamlessly. Developers can build their own parachain tailored to their needs while still benefiting from the security and network effects of the broader Polkadot ecosystem.

While still early in adoption, Polkadot's design addresses the reality that the future is unlikely to be dominated by a single blockchain. Instead, many blockchains will coexist, and Polkadot wants to be the connective tissue between them.

Choosing Tools, Not Sides

Crypto communities often argue about which coin is "the best." But framing it as a zero-sum competition misses the point. Each major cryptocurrency represents a different set of trade-offs.

- **Bitcoin** maximizes security and scarcity.
- **Ethereum** maximizes programmability and flexibility.
- **Litecoin** maximizes familiarity with speed.
- **Cardano** maximizes rigor and sustainability.
- **Solana** maximizes throughput and low fees.
- **BNB Chain** maximizes accessibility and cost-efficiency.
- **Polkadot** maximizes interoperability.
- **XRP Ledger** maximizes settlement speed for financial institutions.
- **Peercoin and Namecoin** remind us that experimentation drives innovation, even if projects fade.

Rather than asking "Which coin wins?," the smarter question is: *Which tool fits this job?* A trader moving funds quickly might choose Solana. An investor seeking long-term scarcity might choose Bitcoin. A developer building a dApp might choose Ethereum or BNB Chain. A global payments company might look to XRP.

The diversity of cryptocurrencies is not a weakness—it's a strength. It shows that the ecosystem is experimenting, evolving, and adapting to different needs.

Closing Thoughts

The story of crypto is not the story of one coin but of many visions running in parallel. Bitcoin provided the spark, Ethereum expanded the canvas, and others explored new designs for speed, sustainability, governance, and interoperability. Together, they form a rich landscape that continues to evolve.

As a beginner, you don't need to master every technical detail of every cryptocurrency. What matters is understanding their roles, their differences, and their trade-offs. This knowledge will help you choose wisely—whether you're investing, building, or simply exploring.

In the next chapter, we'll get even more practical. You'll learn about the best crypto apps, wallets, and exchanges—the essential tools that allow you to actually interact with these cryptocurrencies in the real world.

CHAPTER 6: THE BEST CRYPTO APPS AND EXCHANGES

Entering the World of Crypto Tools

KNOWLEDGE IS POWER, but tools are what turn knowledge into action. If the earlier chapters gave you the "why" of crypto, this one delivers the "how." In practice, you can't interact with cryptocurrency directly—you need apps, wallets, and exchanges to bridge your everyday life with the blockchain. These are your cockpit instruments, the dashboard from which you'll explore the new financial frontier.

For beginners, the sheer variety can be overwhelming. There are thousands of apps, dozens of major exchanges, and a dizzying array of wallets promising security and convenience. Some are trustworthy; others are traps. The goal of this chapter is to give you clarity: to highlight the essential tools, explain their strengths and weaknesses, and help you build a toolkit you can rely on.

By the end, you'll know how to choose an exchange, how wallets actually work, which apps help you track and manage your assets, and what safety practices keep you from falling victim to the common mistakes many newcomers make.

Why Apps and Exchanges Matter

Crypto is a 24/7 global market. Prices shift while you sleep, new tokens launch every day, and scams lurk at every turn. Without the right tools, you're flying blind. With them, you gain transparency, control, and confidence.

Apps are your navigation system: they let you monitor the market, manage your holdings, and access new opportunities like DeFi, NFTs, or staking. Exchanges are your entry and exit points: they convert your fiat money into crypto and vice versa. Wallets are your vaults: they keep your digital gold safe and ensure you—not a third party—control your assets.

Taken together, these tools form your crypto "stack." The better your stack, the smoother your journey.

The Role of Cryptocurrency Exchanges

At the heart of adoption are exchanges—the marketplaces where people buy, sell, and trade crypto. Think of them as digital stock exchanges, but without closing hours or borders. Exchanges make the abstract real: they let you turn dollars, euros, or rand into Bitcoin, Ethereum, or thousands of other tokens.

There are two broad categories: centralized exchanges (CEXs) and decentralized exchanges (DEXs). Understanding their differences is critical.

Centralized Exchanges (CEXs)

Centralized exchanges are run by companies that act as

intermediaries. You create an account, deposit funds, and trade through their platform. They handle liquidity, order matching, and custody (unless you withdraw).

Their advantage is simplicity. Most CEXs offer clean interfaces, mobile apps, and customer support. For many beginners, this is the first stop. Coinbase in the U.S., Luno in parts of Africa, Binance globally—these companies onboard millions of new users every year.

But there are trade-offs. On a CEX, you don't control the private keys to your funds. The exchange holds them on your behalf. This makes it easier to get started, but it introduces trust risk: if the exchange is hacked, mismanaged, or shut down by regulators, your funds may be at risk. The collapse of Mt. Gox in 2014 and the implosion of FTX in 2022 are stark reminders.

Still, for learning the ropes, a CEX is the smoothest on-ramp. It's like training wheels: safe enough to start, but not where you should leave your long-term savings.

Decentralized Exchanges (DEXs)

Decentralized exchanges cut out the middleman. Instead of depositing funds into a company's custody, you connect your wallet directly to smart contracts on the blockchain. Trades happen wallet-to-wallet, governed by code.

This has big advantages: you keep control of your private keys, you don't need to submit identity documents (in most cases), and access is global. Uniswap, PancakeSwap, and SushiSwap are famous examples. On Solana, Jupiter and Raydium fill this role.

But DEXs can intimidate beginners. The interfaces are less polished, the responsibility is higher, and there's no support hotline if you make a mistake. Liquidity can also be lower, meaning larger trades may move the market more.

In short: CEXs are like airports—regulated, centralized, convenient. DEXs are like private runways—permissionless, flexible, but requiring more skill. Most people start on CEXs, then explore DEXs as they gain confidence.

Building Your Crypto Toolkit

Beyond exchanges, a complete crypto toolkit includes wallets and market apps. Each plays a distinct role.

Wallets: Your Keys, Your Coins

A wallet is not where coins live. Coins always live on the blockchain. A wallet is your control panel: it stores the cryptographic keys that prove ownership and lets you sign transactions.

There are two broad categories: hot wallets and cold wallets.

- **Hot wallets** are connected to the internet. They're convenient for everyday use—like carrying cash in your pocket. Trust Wallet, MetaMask, Exodus and Phantom are examples. They're excellent for exploring DeFi or NFTs, but vulnerable if your device is hacked.
- **Cold wallets** keep keys offline. Hardware wallets like Ledger Nano X or Trezor Model T are the gold standard for long-term storage. They add a layer of physical security: even if your computer is compromised, a hacker can't sign transactions without the device in hand.

The golden rule is simple: use hot wallets for small, active funds, and cold wallets for long-term savings. Not your keys, not your coins.

Market Apps: Seeing the Jungle Clearly

Crypto markets are fast-moving jungles. Without a compass, it's easy to get lost in hype. Market apps give you clarity.

- **CoinMarketCap (CMC)** and **CoinGecko** are the two most widely used. They list thousands of coins, track live prices, show trading volumes, and let you compare projects. Checking them daily is a habit for many traders and investors.
- **Portfolio apps** like Blockfolio (now FTX app, later absorbed) or Delta let you track your holdings across wallets and exchanges in one place.
- **News apps** like CoinDesk or The Block keep you updated on events that move markets: regulatory changes, exchange hacks, new token launches.

These apps don't just show numbers. Over time, they teach you to see patterns: which projects are gaining traction, which tokens are trending, and which moves are just noise.

Case Studies: The Apps That Shaped Adoption

Let's look at how a few key apps and exchanges have shaped the way people enter crypto.

- **Coinbase:** Founded in 2012, Coinbase was the first exchange to truly prioritize user experience. Its clean design made buying Bitcoin as easy as buying a book on Amazon. For many Americans, Coinbase was crypto's front door. Its public listing on Nasdaq in 2021 symbolized crypto's arrival in mainstream finance.
- **Binance:** Launched in 2017, Binance grew into the world's largest exchange by volume. Its aggressive listing of new tokens, low fees, and global reach made it wildly popular. It later launched Binance Smart Chain (now BNB Chain), expanding into DeFi and NFTs. Regulatory scrutiny has since intensified, but Binance remains a giant.
- **MetaMask:** A browser extension wallet that opened the door to Ethereum's DeFi boom. Without MetaMask, millions might never have interacted with Uniswap, Aave, or OpenSea. It showed that a wallet could be more than storage—it could be a gateway to an entire decentralized ecosystem.
- **Solflare Wallet:** As Solana rose, Solflare became the default entry point. It combined clean design with access to Solana's dApps and NFTs, onboarding a new wave of users who wanted speed and low fees.

These examples highlight a truth: the tools often shape the adoption curve as much as the technology itself.

Security and Best Practices

Tools are powerful, but they're also dangerous if misused. Many losses in crypto aren't due to blockchain failures—they're due to human mistakes with apps and exchanges.

Here are principles every beginner must internalize:

1. **Never share your seed phrase.** This is the single most important rule. Whoever has it controls your funds. No legitimate service will ever ask for it.
2. **Use two-factor authentication (2FA).** Especially for exchanges. Prefer authenticator apps over SMS.
3. **Start small.** Always test new tools with small amounts before committing real funds.
4. **Don't leave large sums on exchanges.** Exchanges are targets. Use them for trading, not storage.
5. **Verify addresses.** Always double-check the network and destination before sending. A small mistake can mean permanent loss.

How Beginners Can Build Confidence

Your first steps with apps and exchanges are like learning to swim. Start in the shallow end. Download a reputable wallet, write down the seed phrase, and practice receiving a small transfer. Send a tiny amount from an exchange to your wallet and watch it confirm on a block explorer. The thrill of seeing your transaction verified is a powerful confidence booster.

As you grow comfortable, explore more advanced tools—

try a swap on a DEX, experiment with staking a small amount of Ethereum, or mint a low-cost NFT. Each action expands your skill set.

Closing Thoughts

Apps, wallets, and exchanges are the practical layer of crypto. They translate abstract concepts into lived experiences. They're how you go from theory to practice, from curiosity to competence.

Used wisely, they empower you. Used carelessly, they can expose you to risk. The difference lies in habits: test small, guard your keys, diversify your tools, and never stop learning.

In the next chapter, we'll put these tools into action. You'll walk step by step through your first buy and your first sell. You'll learn how to navigate fees, confirmations, and withdrawals. And you'll develop a simple, repeatable process for moving in and out of crypto safely.

Your toolkit is ready. Now it's time to drive.

CHAPTER 7: HOW TO BUY AND SELL CRYPTO

Taking the Leap

UP UNTIL NOW, you've learned what cryptocurrency is, why blockchain matters, and what tools you need to interact with this digital frontier. But there comes a moment when theory must meet practice—when you actually buy your first cryptocurrency.

This is a defining milestone. It's the point at which crypto stops being an abstract concept in a book or a headline in the news and becomes something you own, something you can send, hold, or even trade. The first time you watch your balance update after a transaction, you'll understand the excitement and responsibility that so many people feel in this space.

In this chapter, we'll walk step by step through the process of buying and selling cryptocurrency. We'll look at different methods, explore the pros and cons of each, and explain how to stay safe while doing so. By the end, you'll be able to confidently make your first purchase and understand how to liquidate your assets when the time comes.

Before You Buy: Preparing the Ground

Buying cryptocurrency isn't complicated, but it does require some preparation. Just as you wouldn't walk into the stock market without a brokerage account or a bank without identification, crypto has its own setup steps.

1. **Choose your exchange or platform.** This is where you'll buy your crypto. If you're brand new, a centralized exchange (CEX) like Coinbase, Binance, Kraken, or Bitget is the easiest entry point.
2. **Set up your wallet.** Even if you start by keeping funds on an exchange, you should prepare your own wallet. This could be a hot wallet like Trust Wallet, MetaMask, or Phantom, or a hardware wallet for longer-term storage.
3. **Complete verification.** Most regulated exchanges require Know Your Customer (KYC) checks. Expect to upload an ID, perhaps take a selfie, and wait for approval. It's a one-time process designed to comply with financial regulations.
4. **Fund your account.** Decide how much you're comfortable investing. Use fiat on-ramps (bank transfers, debit/credit cards, or mobile payments) to load funds into your account.

With these steps complete, you're ready to take the plunge.

Method 1: Buying Through a Centralized Exchange

This is the most common way to get your first cryptocurrency. The process is simple:

- **Create and verify your account.** Sign up, complete KYC, and secure your account with two-factor authentication.
- **Deposit fiat currency.** Most exchanges support bank transfers or card payments. You may need to confirm with the bank if it does not work the first time.
- **Select the crypto you want.** Beginners often start with Bitcoin or Ethereum, as they are the most established.
- **Place your order.** You can usually choose between "market orders" (instant purchases at the current price) or "limit orders" (buying at a set price you specify).
- **Withdraw to your wallet (recommended).** While exchanges are convenient, it's safer to withdraw your crypto into a wallet you control.

Centralized exchanges make the process feel familiar, like using an online banking app. The trade-off is trust—you're relying on the exchange to hold your funds securely until you withdraw them.

Method 2: Buying Peer-to-Peer (P2P)

For those who prefer to avoid exchanges or want flexibility in payment methods, peer-to-peer platforms are another option. Here, you buy crypto directly from another person, with the platform acting as an escrow to ensure fairness.

Imagine you want to buy Bitcoin using your local payment app or even cash. On a P2P platform like Binance P2P, Paxful, or LocalBitcoins (now discontinued, but once popular), you browse listings of sellers who accept your preferred method. Once you choose, the platform locks the crypto in escrow. You send payment, and only when the seller confirms receipt is the crypto released to you.

The beauty of P2P is freedom: you can often find local deals, avoid some banking restrictions, and use payment methods unavailable on exchanges. The risk is dealing directly with strangers. That's why escrow services, reputation systems, and platform protections are critical.

Method 3: Buying via Wallet Apps

Some wallets allow you to purchase crypto directly inside the app, often through integrations with services like MoonPay or Simplex. Trust Wallet, Coinbase Wallet, and even MetaMask support this.

This method is convenient because your crypto goes directly into your wallet, skipping the step of transferring from an exchange. But fees are usually higher, and available payment methods vary. It's best for small, quick buys rather than large investments.

Selling Cryptocurrency: Exiting the Market

Buying is exciting, but selling is just as important. Whether you want to lock in profits, cover expenses, or rebalance your portfolio, knowing how to cash out safely is essential.

Selling on Centralized Exchanges

The easiest way is through the same exchange where you bought. Log in, go to the "Sell" section, choose the crypto, and decide whether you want fiat (like USD, EUR, ZAR) or another crypto. Once sold, you can withdraw the fiat to your bank account.

Centralized exchanges are the smoothest off-ramp for most people. They handle the conversion and regulatory compliance for you.

Selling Peer-to-Peer

Just like buying, you can also sell via P2P. You list your crypto for sale, set terms, and wait for a buyer. The platform holds your crypto in escrow until payment arrives. This method can sometimes give you better rates or access to local currencies that exchanges don't support.

Selling via Wallet Apps

Wallets that allow purchases often also allow sales. This usually involves selling crypto for fiat, which is then transferred to your bank or card. Again, convenience is the selling point, but fees can be steep.

Common Pitfalls to Avoid

Newcomers often make the same mistakes when buying or selling crypto. Here are some traps to avoid:

- **Overinvesting too quickly.** Always start small. The market is volatile, and rushing in with large amounts can lead to regret.
- **Leaving funds on exchanges.** Exchanges can be hacked or freeze withdrawals. Withdraw to your own wallet when possible.
- **Falling for scams.** Fake exchanges, fraudulent sellers, and too-good-to-be-true offers are common. Stick with reputable platforms.
- **Ignoring fees.** Every method has fees—whether hidden in spreads or explicit transaction costs. Compare before you commit.
- **Using the wrong network.** When withdrawing, make sure you're using the correct blockchain (e.g., don't send Ethereum tokens to a Bitcoin address).

A Practical Walkthrough: Your First Purchase

Let's imagine you're a beginner who wants to buy $100 worth of Bitcoin using Binance. Here's how it might look:

1. Sign up for Binance and complete verification.
2. Secure your account with 2FA.
3. Deposit $100 using a debit card.
4. Navigate to the "Buy" section, select Bitcoin, and confirm a purchase at market price.
5. Instantly, your balance shows around 0.0017 BTC (depending on the market).
6. You withdraw the BTC to your hardware wallet.

> The network confirms the transaction, and now you hold Bitcoin in self-custody.

That's it—you're officially a crypto owner. From here, you could hold it long-term, trade it, or even send it across the globe in minutes.

Selling Scenario

Months later, Bitcoin's price has risen, and your $100 investment is now worth $200. You decide to sell half. You log into Binance, select "Sell," choose $100 worth of Bitcoin, and withdraw the fiat to your bank. The transaction takes a day or two to clear, and just like that, you've realized a profit.

The Bigger Picture

Buying and selling isn't just about profit—it's about participation. Every time you buy, you're signaling belief in the future of blockchain. Every time you sell, you're testing the system's ability to bridge crypto and the traditional economy.

As adoption grows, these processes will become faster, cheaper, and more seamless. Already, we see crypto debit cards that let you spend directly at shops, wallets that integrate bank-like services, and countries experimenting with central bank digital currencies (CBDCs).

Today, buying and selling are conscious processes. Tomorrow, it may feel as normal as swiping a card.

Key Takeaways

- Buying crypto can be done through centralized exchanges, peer-to-peer platforms, or wallet apps.
- Selling follows the same logic, with centralized exchanges offering the easiest fiat withdrawals.
- Always start small, use reputable platforms, and secure your assets in personal wallets.
- Buying and selling is more than a transaction—it's your entry into the decentralized future.

Preparing for What's Next

Now that you know how to enter and exit the crypto market, the next logical question is what to do with your holdings. Should you trade actively, seeking to profit from daily swings? Or should you hold long-term, trusting in the steady rise of adoption?

That's what the next chapter will tackle: **Trading and Holding.** You'll discover the differences between these strategies, the psychology behind them, and how they shape the entire crypto market.

Your first purchase may be the spark—but how you manage it determines whether that spark grows into lasting success.

CHAPTER 8: TRADING AND HOLDING

Two Paths, One Goal

OWNING cryptocurrency is only the beginning. Once you've bought your first Bitcoin, Ethereum, or Solana, the next question arises: *what do you do with it?* Do you hold onto it, waiting patiently for its value to rise over the years? Or do you actively trade, buying and selling in an attempt to capture profit from the market's constant fluctuations?

This chapter is about these two central strategies—**trading** and **holding** (often called "HODLing"). Each approach has its own philosophy, risks, and rewards. Together, they form the backbone of the crypto economy. Traders keep markets liquid and prices dynamic, while holders provide stability and long-term confidence.

By the end of this chapter, you'll understand both strategies in depth, their psychological demands, and how to decide which (or what mix) is right for you.

The Nature of the Crypto Market

Before diving into the strategies themselves, it's important to understand what makes the crypto market unique. Unlike traditional stock exchanges that open and close daily, the cryptocurrency market never sleeps. It operates 24 hours a day, 7 days a week, 365 days a year. This constant activity creates both opportunity and stress.

The market is also known for its **extreme volatility**. A cryptocurrency's price can rise or fall 20% in a single day—movements that would be considered earth-shattering in traditional finance. This volatility is the trader's playground and the holder's test of patience.

Another defining feature is **global participation**. Anyone, anywhere, with an internet connection can trade or invest in crypto. This openness contributes to wild swings in sentiment, as millions of individuals and institutions act simultaneously, often reacting to news, rumors, and emotions.

With this backdrop in mind, let's explore the two main approaches.

Trading: The Active Path

Trading is the art of buying and selling assets to profit from price movements. In crypto, traders take advantage of volatility, analyzing charts, patterns, and market sentiment to make quick decisions.

Styles of Trading

Trading isn't one-size-fits-all. There are several distinct approaches, each with its own rhythm:

- **Day Trading** involves buying and selling within a single day, sometimes in just hours or minutes. Day traders live by charts and price alerts, constantly scanning for opportunities. It's high risk, high stress, and requires discipline.
- **Swing Trading** is a medium-term strategy. Swing traders hold positions for several days or weeks, aiming to capture "swings" in price trends. They balance technical analysis (charts) with broader market narratives.
- **Scalping** takes things to an extreme, with traders executing dozens or even hundreds of small trades in a single day. Each trade may yield only tiny profits, but the volume adds up. This method demands precision and access to platforms with very low fees.
- **Position Trading** is long-term trading. Here, traders look at the bigger picture—market cycles, adoption trends, and macroeconomics—and hold positions for months or years. While it resembles holding, the mindset is different: position traders still look for the best entry and exit points, guided by analysis.

Each style requires not only skill but also emotional control. The crypto market's volatility can quickly turn profits into losses. Successful traders master not just strategies but also psychology.

The Trader's Toolbox

Traders rely on a range of tools to make decisions:

- **Charts and Technical Analysis**: Candlestick charts, moving averages, RSI (Relative Strength Index), MACD (Moving Average Convergence Divergence), and Fibonacci retracements are all part of the trader's toolkit. These indicators help identify momentum, reversals, and support/resistance levels.
- **News and Sentiment**: A tweet from a billionaire, a regulatory announcement, or the launch of a new project can spark massive price moves. Traders track these events closely, often reacting within minutes.
- **Exchanges and Interfaces**: Platforms like Binance, Bybit, Bitget, and Kraken offer advanced trading features such as leverage, derivatives, and futures. While these tools can amplify profits, they can also magnify losses.

THE CHALLENGES OF TRADING

Trading sounds glamorous, but in reality, it is grueling work. Most beginners lose money because they underestimate the difficulty of competing against experienced traders and even algorithmic bots.

Key challenges include:

- **Emotional Control**: Fear and greed drive bad decisions. Selling too early out of fear or buying at the peak from FOMO (fear of missing out) are classic mistakes.

- **Time Commitment**: Active trading demands constant attention and quick reactions. It's not compatible with everyone's lifestyle.
- **Risk of Overleveraging**: Some traders use borrowed money (leverage) to magnify their positions. While this can increase gains, it can also wipe out an account in minutes.

Despite these risks, successful traders do exist. They thrive because they treat trading as a profession, with rules, strategies, and discipline.

Holding (HODLing): The Passive Path

On the opposite side of the spectrum is **holding**, often called **HODLing** thanks to a legendary typo in a 2013 Bitcoin forum post where a user declared "I AM HODLING" during a market crash. The word stuck, and today it represents long-term conviction.

HODLers don't worry about daily fluctuations. Instead, they buy and hold crypto for years, believing that adoption, scarcity, and technological progress will drive long-term growth.

The Philosophy of Holding

Holding isn't about timing the market. It's about believing in the fundamentals of blockchain technology and the trajectory of adoption. Holders argue that:

- **Time in the market beats timing the market.** Missing even a few of the best-performing days in crypto can drastically reduce long-term returns.
- **Volatility is noise.** Short-term drops may look scary, but zooming out shows that Bitcoin, Ethereum, and other major cryptocurrencies have historically trended upward.
- **Scarcity drives value.** Bitcoin's capped supply of 21 million coins makes it a deflationary asset. Over time, demand increases while supply remains fixed.

This strategy requires patience and emotional resilience. Watching your portfolio drop 50% in a bear market is painful, but HODLers see it as part of the journey.

The Holder's Toolkit

While holders don't spend their days analyzing charts, they still need to take key precautions:

- **Cold Storage**: Hardware wallets like Ledger or Trezor are essential for keeping assets safe over the long term.
- **Diversification**: Many holders spread their investments across major assets like Bitcoin, Ethereum, and a few promising altcoins to reduce risk.
- **Education**: Staying informed about the crypto landscape helps holders maintain conviction through downturns.

. . .

THE REWARDS AND RISKS OF HOLDING

The rewards of holding are evident in stories of early Bitcoin adopters. Someone who bought a few hundred dollars' worth in 2011 and held on is likely sitting on millions today. But holding is not without risk.

- **Emotional Strain**: Bear markets can last years, testing even the most faithful holders.
- **Opportunity Cost**: While holding, you may miss out on gains from trading or newer projects.
- **Security Responsibility**: If you mismanage your private keys or wallet backups, no one can help you recover lost funds.

Still, for many beginners, holding remains the safest and most realistic strategy.

Trading vs. Holding: A Comparison

Both approaches have their place, and both shape the crypto market in powerful ways.

- **Traders** provide liquidity, making it easy for others to buy or sell. They create volatility, which attracts attention and media coverage.
- **Holders** create stability by locking up supply. Their conviction often supports prices during downturns and provides a foundation for long-term adoption.

The truth is that the healthiest markets need both. Without traders, markets stagnate. Without holders, markets collapse under their own volatility.

A Hybrid Approach

Many investors choose a middle path, combining elements of both strategies. For example, they may hold a "core" portfolio of Bitcoin and Ethereum for the long term while actively trading a smaller portion of their funds to capture short-term opportunities.

This hybrid strategy offers balance: the security of long-term growth plus the excitement (and potential profits) of trading. It also allows beginners to experiment with trading while keeping most of their portfolio safe.

Lessons from History

History shows the strengths and weaknesses of both strategies.

- During the **2017 bull run**, traders made fortunes by riding volatile altcoins. But many lost just as quickly when the market crashed in 2018. Holders who stayed the course, however, eventually saw new all-time highs in 2021.
- In the **2020–2021 cycle**, day traders capitalized on DeFi and NFT booms, while holders of Bitcoin and Ethereum saw their portfolios multiply. Those who sold too early often regretted missing the explosive upside.

- Conversely, during **crypto winters**, holders endured years of losses, while skilled traders could profit from shorting or playing small price ranges.

The lesson: no strategy is foolproof. Success depends on your goals, temperament, and time horizon.

Key Takeaways

- Trading is active, demanding, and high-risk, offering quick gains (or losses).
- Holding is passive, patient, and focused on long-term adoption and growth.
- Both approaches shape the market—traders drive liquidity, holders provide stability.
- A hybrid strategy allows you to benefit from both without going "all in" on one method.

Building Toward the Next Chapter

Now that you've learned the strategies of managing crypto, it's time to tackle one of the most important topics in your journey: **security**. Owning and managing crypto means becoming your own bank. With that freedom comes responsibility—and countless threats.

In the next chapter, we'll dive into **Crypto Security**, covering scams, hacks, and best practices to protect your digital wealth. If you master security, you'll not only safeguard your investments but also gain the confidence to explore the crypto world more boldly.

CHAPTER 9: CRYPTO SECURITY

Why Security is the Cornerstone of Crypto

UP TO THIS POINT, you've learned what crypto is, how to buy and sell it, and how to manage your assets through trading or holding. But none of that matters if your funds aren't safe. In traditional finance, banks, regulators, and insurance companies provide layers of protection. If your card is stolen or your bank is hacked, you often get your money back.

Crypto is different. You are your own bank. This is empowering—but it also makes you your own last line of defense. Once your funds are stolen, there is almost no way to recover them.

That's why understanding crypto security is essential. In this chapter, we'll cover the main threats in the crypto world, real stories of hacks and scams, and the best practices every beginner must follow to keep their assets safe. By the end, you'll not only know how to recognize dangers but also how to build strong defenses.

The Landscape of Crypto Threats

The crypto industry has attracted innovators, entrepreneurs, and investors—but also scammers, hackers, and criminals. Billions of dollars have been lost to hacks and scams since Bitcoin's creation.

Unlike losing your credit card, where you can call the bank, in crypto, the responsibility is entirely on you. The threats are many: phishing websites, fake apps, malicious wallets, rug pulls, exchange hacks, and even simple mistakes like sending funds to the wrong address.

To prepare you, let's examine the most common attack vectors.

Common Scams and Hacks in Crypto

1. Phishing Attacks

Phishing is one of the oldest tricks in the book, and in crypto, it's everywhere. Hackers create fake websites or apps that look identical to real ones. You think you're logging into your exchange account, but instead, you're handing your username, password, and even two-factor codes to scammers.

They also send emails or messages pretending to be from "Binance Support" or "MetaMask Team," urging you to click links and confirm details.

Case in Point: In 2021, scammers created a fake version

of Uniswap's website. Thousands of users connected their wallets, unknowingly granting permission for attackers to drain their funds.

How to Protect Yourself:

- Always type the website address manually or use bookmarks.
- Double-check for subtle spelling changes in URLs.
- Never enter your seed phrase online.

2. Fake Airdrops and Giveaways

"Send us 1 ETH and we'll send you back 2!"

This scam has been circulating for years, often promoted by fake social media accounts impersonating celebrities or projects.

The formula is simple: scammers create fake Twitter accounts, Telegram groups, or YouTube livestreams claiming to give away free tokens. Victims send funds, expecting double, but receive nothing.

Case in Point: A fake Elon Musk giveaway on Twitter once stole over $2 million worth of crypto in just a few days.

How to Protect Yourself:

- Never send funds expecting a larger return.
- Verify official social media channels through project websites.
- Remember: legitimate airdrops don't require you to send money.

. . .

3. Rug Pulls and Scam Tokens

In the world of DeFi and meme coins, new tokens appear daily. Some are genuine experiments, but many are traps. Developers hype their project, attract investors, and then disappear—taking the liquidity with them. This is called a **rug pull**.

Case in Point: In 2021, a token inspired by the Netflix series *Squid Game* went viral. Its price skyrocketed, but when investors tried to sell, they couldn't. The developers had coded the token to prevent selling. Days later, they cashed out and vanished, stealing over $3 million.

How to Protect Yourself:

- Research the team behind the project—anonymous teams can be risky.
- Check if liquidity is locked (reputable projects often lock it for months or years).
- Look for third-party audits of the code.

4. Exchange Hacks

Even the biggest exchanges have been hacked. When exchanges store billions in user funds, they become prime targets.

Case in Point: Mt. Gox, once the world's largest Bitcoin exchange, collapsed in 2014 after losing 850,000 BTC to hackers. More recently, in 2019, Binance was hacked for 7,000 BTC, though they refunded users from their insurance fund.

How to Protect Yourself:

- Never keep large amounts of crypto on exchanges.
- Use them only for trading, then withdraw to your personal wallet.
- Choose exchanges with proof-of-reserves and strong security reputations.

5. Malware and Keyloggers

Hackers can infect your computer or phone with malware that records everything you type. If you enter your seed phrase or private key, it's game over. Some malware even replaces copied wallet addresses with the hacker's address.

Case in Point: A user intending to send 0.5 BTC to a friend copied the address from their wallet. Unknown to them, malware on their computer swapped the address. They pasted and confirmed the transaction, sending funds straight to a hacker.

How to Protect Yourself:

- Keep your operating system and antivirus software updated.
- Double-check wallet addresses character by character.
- Use a dedicated device for crypto if possible.

6. Impersonation Scams

Scammers often pose as customer support agents. You ask for help on Twitter or Telegram, and a "support representative" messages you, asking for your private key or to screenshare.

Case in Point: Countless MetaMask users have lost funds after being tricked by fake "support" accounts offering assistance.

How to Protect Yourself:

- Real support teams will never ask for private keys.
- Only use official websites or help desks.
- Never allow strangers remote access to your device.

Best Practices for Crypto Security

Now that we've outlined the threats, let's go through the defensive playbook. These practices form the foundation of safe crypto management.

1. Master Your Keys and Seed Phrases

Your private keys and seed phrases are the crown jewels. Anyone who has them has complete control of your funds.

- Write your seed phrase on paper and store it securely.
- Consider using metal seed storage for fire and water resistance.
- Never save it in cloud storage or screenshots.

2. Use Hardware Wallets for Long-Term Storage

Hardware wallets, also called cold wallets, are devices that store your keys offline. This makes them nearly immune to hacking.

Popular options include Ledger Nano X, Trezor Model T, ColdCard, and Ellipal Titan.

For long-term holding, nothing beats hardware wallets.

3. Enable Strong Authentication

Add extra layers of security:

- Use two-factor authentication (2FA) with apps like Authy or Google Authenticator.
- Avoid SMS-based 2FA, as SIM-swapping attacks are common.
- Use unique, strong passwords for every exchange or wallet.

4. Separate Devices for Crypto

Consider using a dedicated phone or computer for crypto transactions. By limiting exposure to daily browsing, social media, and downloads, you reduce the chance of malware infection.

5. Stay Updated and Informed

The crypto landscape evolves rapidly, and so do scams. By

staying plugged into reputable news sources and communities, you'll recognize red flags early.

Knowledge is your best shield.

The Human Factor

While technology provides tools, the biggest vulnerability in crypto is human error. Many hacks succeed not because of code flaws but because users made simple mistakes—clicking the wrong link, storing keys insecurely, or acting out of greed.

Security in crypto isn't just about devices and wallets; it's about mindset. Caution, skepticism, and patience are your allies.

Lessons from History

- **Mt. Gox (2014):** Taught the community never to leave funds on centralized exchanges.
- **The DAO Hack (2016):** Exposed vulnerabilities in smart contracts and led to Ethereum's split into ETH and ETC.
- **Ledger Data Breach (2020):** Highlighted the need to protect not just funds but also personal data. Customers' addresses and phone numbers were leaked, leading to phishing attacks.

Each event reshaped the industry, reinforcing one truth: security must always come first.

Building Toward the Final Chapter

You now know the threats, the tactics of scammers, and the tools to protect yourself. With this knowledge, you're ready to move forward with confidence.

In the final chapter, **Your Crypto Journey Begins**, we'll tie everything together—mindset, tools, strategies, and security—into a roadmap for your future in crypto. This is where your preparation meets action.

CHAPTER 10: YOUR CRYPTO JOURNEY BEGINS

The Road So Far

YOU STARTED this book as someone curious about cryptocurrency. Maybe you'd heard about Bitcoin on the news, or maybe a friend mentioned Ethereum, or perhaps you stumbled across a viral tweet about NFTs or Solana. At first, crypto might have felt overwhelming—technical jargon, wild price swings, and a stream of scams and headlines.

But chapter by chapter, you've built a foundation:

- You learned the history of money and why Bitcoin was born.
- You explored wallets, transactions, and blockchains.
- You studied the fundamentals—decentralization, cryptography, consensus, and tokenomics.
- You discovered the leading cryptocurrencies and how each fills a different niche.

- You got practical with exchanges, apps, and wallets.
- You walked step by step through buying and selling.
- You explored trading and holding strategies, learning the balance between activity and patience.
- You understood why security is the single most important skill in crypto.

Now, you are ready to begin your journey—not as an outsider looking in, but as a participant in the next evolution of finance.

Crypto as a Journey, Not a Destination

One of the biggest misconceptions about crypto is that there's a "finish line." Buy the right coin, hold it, and retire. That's a fantasy. In reality, crypto is a constantly moving frontier. New projects appear, old ones fade; technology improves, regulations evolve.

That's why the best way to think about your role in crypto is as a **traveler**. A traveler doesn't expect to reach every destination at once. They explore, learn, make mistakes, and grow.

Your crypto journey will look different from others. Some people become traders, some builders, some collectors, some investors. Some dive deep into DeFi, others focus on Bitcoin as digital gold. The key is to know your path and move with intention.

Building the Right Mindset

More than any technical skill, mindset determines success in crypto.

1. Patience and Perspective

Crypto markets are volatile. There will be weeks where your portfolio soars, and weeks where it crashes. The patient investor zooms out. Bitcoin has fallen more than 80% several times—but long-term holders still came out ahead. Patience beats panic.

2. Curiosity and Continuous Learning

Crypto changes fast. Ethereum didn't exist until 2015. NFTs exploded in 2021. Layer-2 scaling solutions are only just beginning. What you know today is valuable, but it's never enough for tomorrow. The people who thrive are lifelong learners.

3. Responsibility and Discipline

Crypto gives you freedom—no bank can freeze your funds, no government can inflate your Bitcoin supply. But with freedom comes responsibility. You are your own bank, your own security guard, your own record-keeper. Discipline protects you from careless mistakes.

Your First Steps Beyond This Book

Reading alone isn't enough. To really learn crypto, you need to use it. Here's a practical roadmap for your first months:

1. **Set Up a Wallet**
    - Install a hot wallet like MetaMask, Phantom, or Trust Wallet.

- Write down your seed phrase securely and test restoring it.

2. **Buy Your First Crypto**
   - Start with a small purchase—enough to learn, but not enough to hurt if you make a mistake.
   - Buy Bitcoin, Ethereum, or Solana on a trusted exchange, then withdraw to your wallet.
3. **Make a Transaction**
   - Send a small amount to a friend or another of your wallets.
   - Watch it confirm on a block explorer—seeing your transaction on-chain is a powerful moment.
4. **Explore the Ecosystem**
   - Try swapping tokens on a decentralized exchange.
   - Stake some coins and watch rewards accumulate.
   - Mint or buy a small NFT just to experience the process.
5. **Level Up Security**
   - Buy a hardware wallet.
   - Move long-term holdings into cold storage.
   - Practice using 2FA and secure backups.

Each of these steps will teach you more than hours of reading ever could.

Pitfalls to Avoid Early On

As you step into the crypto world, keep in mind the mistakes most beginners make:

- **Chasing hype.** Don't buy a coin just because it's trending on Twitter.
- **Ignoring fees.** Network fees can eat into small transactions; always check before confirming.
- **Neglecting security.** If you leave all your funds on an exchange or store your seed phrase in your email, it's only a matter of time before disaster strikes.
- **Going all in.** Never invest more than you can afford to lose. Crypto should be part of a balanced financial plan, not your entire plan.

The Broader Vision

Crypto isn't just about making money. At its core, it's about freedom, transparency, and inclusion. It's about enabling people in Argentina to escape hyperinflation, freelancers in Nigeria to get paid without middlemen, or artists in Indonesia to sell digital art globally.

It's about building systems that don't depend on trust in one company or government but are verifiable by anyone, anywhere. In many ways, crypto is less about technology and more about human coordination.

If the first internet democratized information, this one democratizes value.

Where the Future Might Take You

This book is your launchpad, but your journey could lead to many frontiers:

- **DeFi (Decentralized Finance):** Lending, borrowing, trading, and investing without intermediaries.
- **NFTs (Non-Fungible Tokens):** Digital ownership for art, games, and beyond.
- **DAOs (Decentralized Autonomous Organizations):** Online communities that govern and allocate capital.
- **Layer-2 Scaling:** Faster, cheaper blockchains that extend Ethereum's reach.
- **Web3 Apps:** Social networks, games, and tools where you own your data.
- **Regulation and Policy:** Helping shape laws that will define how the world adopts crypto.

No one can explore everything, but you can choose a path that excites you.

A Final Word of Encouragement

You are early. Most people still don't understand crypto. They think it's a fad, a scam, or something too complicated for "normal" people. But so did most people in the 1990s about the internet.

By reading this book, you've placed yourself ahead of the

curve. You've armed yourself with the knowledge to avoid traps, seize opportunities, and participate in shaping the future of money.

There will be mistakes. You might lose a small amount to a bad swap, forget a memo once, or panic-sell during a dip. That's normal. What matters is that you learn, adapt, and keep going.

Crypto rewards persistence.

Parting Thoughts

This book was never meant to give you every answer. It was meant to give you a foundation strong enough to start and to continue learning on your own.

The truth is, no book, course, or mentor can prepare you for everything you'll encounter. The market changes, the technology evolves, and new risks and opportunities appear every year. What will carry you forward is your mindset: curiosity, discipline, patience, and courage.

The future of finance is being written now—on blockchains, by people like you. By starting your journey today, you're not just investing in coins; you're investing in a new system of value, ownership, and trust.

So take your first steps with confidence. Buy that first fraction of Bitcoin. Send your first transaction. Explore your first DeFi app. Learn by doing.

The crypto world is vast, exciting, and sometimes dangerous—but it's also full of opportunity for those who prepare.

Your journey begins here.

All the Blessings

Nadav Sananes - Author & Project Founder

Netanel Sananes - Project Manager

www.ingramcontent.com/pod-product-compliance
Lightning Source LLC
LaVergne TN
LVHW022009200926
848481LV00007B/2307

* 9 7 9 8 9 0 2 2 2 2 7 9 8 *